Foresight: Finding Your Footing in a Fast-Forward World

Cover design by Tylar Masters of Tylar & Co.
Editing and formatting by Amanda E. Clark of Grammar Chic, Inc.

ISBN 978-0985571252

Published by Top Tier Leadership, P.O. Box 30846, Palm Beach Gardens, Florida 33420

NOTE: While the author has made every effort to provide accurate Internet addresses in the endnotes at the time of publication, neither the publisher nor the author assumes any responsibility for errors, or for changes that occur after publication. Further, author and publisher do not have any control over and does not assume responsibility for third-party Web sites or their content.

For more information or to make a media inquiry, please visit www.toptierleadership.com.

DEDICATION

To my husband, Steve—You are my everything.

To our son, Addison—Create the life you desire.

TABLE OF CONTENTS

FORESIGHT:
FINDING YOUR FOOTING IN A FAST-FORWARD WORLD

by

Rita Barreto Craig, SPHR, SHRM-SCP

TOP TIER
LEADERSHIP

www.toptierleadership.com

PREFACE

Looking Back . . .

Some old sayings are never really old:

"If only I knew then what I know now."

"Hindsight is 20/20."

Countless anecdotes and catchy quips are used to describe the folly of youth and the importance of progressively-acquired experience. And there are certain points in life when catchphrases seem especially poignant: a significant birthday, the arrival of a second or third child, a promotion, an approaching retirement.

Gazing at the professional woman peering out from Kathy's mirror, it was hard to fathom that it was the same person who entered the workforce nearly forty years ago as a buoyant, wide-eyed secretary. It had been four decades of climbing the corporate ladder, from secretary to office manager to operations director, then all the way up to executive vice president. It had been a truly groundbreaking career, especially for a woman who entered the workforce in the early 1970s; definitely a career to be proud of.

And one that now would end in the blink of an eye.

"Today, that career ends," she said quietly to herself.

As Kathy slipped her feet into a pair of heels, all of her energy was focused on her last day of work, and she was feeling myriad emotions. She was excited for what was to come, and there was no denying she had many questions about the journey. But she

1

was also thinking about what was ending, and how, for better or worse, it had shaped her.

Today's working world was a different place than the one she had entered forty years ago right out of college. She was proud of all she had accomplished, especially while holding several job titles—wife, mother, business professional. She had done many things right, but there were also some things, that, given the chance, she would have done differently.

"No regrets," Kathy said to her reflection, "I only have advice on how to do even better than I did." She had been vocal on this point, especially to her kids as they started their own careers. With them, she had stressed lessons about having a fulfilling professional and personal life, while sometimes figuring out firsthand about what *not* to do.

Kathy hoped they would take her instruction. She was only offering help from a place of experience. After all, who better to advise on what's important to professional success than the person who is about to leave it behind?

What Do I Do NOW?

Kyle sat down at the breakfast table, as he had done every day for years. He didn't have much of an appetite, but he couldn't disappoint Maggie, who was buzzing with excitement.

"Ready for your last day on the job?" she chirped, placing a spoonful of scrambled eggs on his plate and passing the bacon. "What time did you say the party started again?"

Taking a slice, Kyle thanked her for her efforts and said, "Six o'clock." He was excited about the party that evening, but also a bit scared. Apparently it showed.

"You okay?" Maggie asked, concern etched on her face.

Kyle shrugged. "Yeah, I suppose so. Just can't believe this day is really here."

That earned him a smile from his wife and a congratulatory pat

2

on the shoulder. "Well, you should be proud. It's quite an accomplishment. Forty-four years in the working world. You've earned a great send-off, and now you can just take it easy."

Kyle swallowed hard.

"Taking it easy." That's *exactly* what was making him feel nervous. He knew he had reached a huge milestone, making it to retirement. It's just that the question of "what do I do now?" loomed over his head like the proverbial Sword of Damocles.

He had had a successful career. He was accomplished in his field and had done a good job. A *damn* good job. But . . .

And that's where the issue was. Sure, he had a great wife, three grown kids who all had families and careers of their own. By all intents and purposes he was living the American Dream. Right down to the white picket fence outside. The problem was that for the past forty-four years, his career had consumed him, and starting tomorrow morning there would be hours in the day that he wasn't sure how to fill. What does a person do when they suddenly lose the focus of their life?

Kyle had of course been a good husband and attentive father. But he was only now realizing that those things had always operated on the periphery of his life. Any hobby he might have enjoyed were just extensions of his professional self. His need to climb the corporate ladder had always defined him.

And that was about to change.

"So what is it that you would like to do tomorrow?" smiled Maggie as she sat down across the table from him.

Kyle looked down at his plate and then up at his wife.

"I don't know," he said, realizing for the first time in his adult life that he didn't have a schedule to keep or somewhere to be. With a jolt, he also understood it was a question he might have to answer every day for the rest of his life.

CHAPTER 1

Purposefully vs. Purposely

It's easy to assume that people on the cusp of retirement—moving on to the next stage of life after hanging up their professional hats—are eager and happy to "clock out" for the last time with barely a look back. This is *part of it,* of course, and it's my experience that this assumption is most often held by the young; those who are looking forward toward their career, not backward.

It's a fact that any accomplished individual who has worked toward that moment faces myriad emotions, not just about what happens next, but about *what just happened.* And it's the reason that I was inspired to write this book.

My tome is not aimed at the seasoned worker, the person who has already run the gamut of their career and sees the horizon clearly, but rather for the new professional, the person with emerging dreams, goals, and professional desires. This is the group that needs to take a moment and understand what they have *right now* in order to plan for what they will have in twenty, thirty, or forty years. Someone beginning or continuing a professional journey can't simply go through the day-to-day motions focusing on getting the job done. Too many people who have done that live to regret it.

If you're one of those at the starting line, think about what not only pleases you right now, but what you want from the future. Think about the end. Picture it, live it today, and of course, enjoy it. Your life and career are not a dress rehearsal, so don't treat it as such.

Planning for Your Curtain Call

It may appear challenging to plan for both your short- and long-term future when just starting out. As a Baby Boomer professional who got her feet wet in the corporate world in the 1960s and 70s, I have worked with so many individuals who are like Kathy and Kyle. Their stories are not unique. So many people fail to slow down and stop during their careers to engage in what they want to do on a methodical level, realizing they have acquired certain types of knowledge but can't utilize that experience and wisdom now as they are considering their careers in hindsight.

Kathy might fall into that group, but what's worse is the number of people like Kyle. They're the overachievers, the workaholics, those who focus so intently on the day-to-day of their career that they are unable to look at themselves as more than that. They believe they're working to achieve the American Dream, and nothing is going to get in their way—at least until their only hobby, their work, is shrinking like the setting sun in the rearview mirror.

It's so necessary these days for young people to understand that their career, their life, and their future are not mutually exclusive. If you're a member of this group, know that your existence is a living, breathing, morphing being. You can't put it on autopilot now and expect to be happy down the road. You must plan for your own curtain call. Doing so now, strategically, will help you get the most out of your career, your retirement, and your life.

Not Just another Book about Retirement

When I started thinking about what I wanted to convey in this book, I knew I didn't simply want to write about retirement or how to have a successful career. That's been done over and over. Most books focus on the present looking forward. None look backward from the future, from a place of experience. So that's what I decided to do.

I will instruct you, the reader, on all the things you must be doing now, professionally and personally, so you are set up for success, not only today but thirty or forty years down the line. My goal: That you finish this book with clear ideas about what you need to begin implementing now in order to have an enjoyable career and personal life and be ready for retirement. I want you to sleep at night without worrying about "what comes next?"

I will coach you from a place of experience, as a professional woman and mentor who made it to retirement and then looked back to assess what I did right, and what I did that wasn't so right. I will give you the tools to know the difference between living your life purposefully versus purposely.

CHAPTER 2

A Healthy Sense of Curiosity

"I have no special talents. I am only passionately curious."

Those words, delivered by Albert Einstein, are particularly poignant, especially when people consider their career, their outside interests, what drives them, and who they are, now and in the future. Having a healthy sense of curiosity is powerful and comes coupled with the ability to shape one's life for the better.

What does it mean to be curious? How can it affect your retirement?

It matters because if you don't develop and hone a curious nature early on, you are liable to become like Kyle when you face retirement, and what then? If you haven't taken the time to stay interested in the world around you, to explore and inquire and become more than a two-dimensional worker punching in and out each day, you will face some very empty time when a job no longer fills your hours.

Think about it. Kyle is realizing that he spent the last forty years chasing the American dream, climbing the corporate ladder, only to discover that he never developed an interest in anything else. He has no idea what the next day will bring because he didn't spend any time envisioning it or developing interests so he could become someone other than "Kyle the working man."

Many people might scoff at this idea and identify with Kyle. After all, who has time for outside activities and interests when working a sixty hour week, trying to get ahead? Let me counter your claim with this: I chose the quote from Albert Einstein because it relates to his introspection and assessment of curiosity. He was also known for saying, "The important thing is not to stop questioning . . . Never lose a holy curiosity."

Einstein wasn't alone in his analysis of the important role curiosity plays in our lives. Thomas Edison, Leonardo da Vinci, Richard Feynman, Marie Curie, and Plato all promoted their curiosity avidly and I doubt that any of these geniuses ever used working long hours as an excuse to go intellectually and mentally stagnant. I suspect they very rarely sat around twiddling their thumbs trying to figure out what to do next, the exact conundrum Kyle is facing.

Too many professionals put all their time and energy into planning the day-to-day while they are working, waiting until the twilight of their careers to contemplate what else interests and inspires them. Then they come up short because they've never opened their mind to other possibilities. They've had plenty of *thoughts* about tomorrow, but never taken any action:

"Tomorrow I'm going to start training for a marathon."
"Tomorrow I'm going to learn to speak Japanese."
"Tomorrow I'm going to take salsa lessons with my husband."
"Tomorrow I'm going to (fill in the blank)."

Such thoughts mean nothing if you don't make them a priority, acting on them throughout your career.

Keeping an Open Mind

It's one thing to be positive and upbeat while in the workplace. It's another thing to carry that with you once five o'clock (or later) hits. So many people fall into a rut, pushing full speed ahead while working only to turn off their brains when they return home.

I can't caution strongly enough against this behavior. Keeping an open mind is a core component of developing a sense of curiosity throughout life and is essential to being happy in retirement. It's how you prevent becoming a hobby-less, interest-less, hopeless person like Kyle when your career ends.

So how do you keep an open mind? It might sound like an easy thing to do, but many people, young and old, get it wrong. First, be open to learning new things, unlearning old information or behaviors, and replacing them with new knowledge and interests. This allows you to inject change and variety into your life. It will help you discover what makes you tick outside your chosen profession and keep your mind active, engaged, and zealous. It will help prevent the cobwebs from settling in and keep you from becoming irrelevant.

Curious Minds Don't Take Things for Granted

Life should not be about simply accepting the status quo. Well-rounded people dig deeper, both in their personal and professional lives. They develop the ability to see more, experience new things, and live a richer life. They benefit because, unlike Kyle, they don't have a singular focus.

Having this capability also makes them more valuable to the people around them. Those who aren't ready to accept things "as is" in their life are going to push faster and harder at the office. They are going to be the go-getters that a manager or business owner wants on their team because their passion extends far beyond simply doing what their job description requires. They also tend to be more efficient and can look at a situation from multiple angles. They discover superior solutions, have improved productivity, and comprehend details better compared to their peers.

Additionally, people who dig deeper are constantly putting

themselves outside of their comfort zone. They expose themselves to more opportunities and to people who are components of a rich existence. And when this happens, it becomes very hard to ever use the words, "I'm bored."

Stop Using the "B" Word

That leads to my next point about developing and sustaining a curious mind. Truly inquisitive, thoughtful people never ever say, "I'm bored," or "This is boring." While life can't always be a thrill a minute, having a curious mind definitely helps prevent the creep of boredom and tedium. And realize that the moment you say those words, you close the door on whatever possibility could have been in front of you.

Feeling bored is a state of mind. Our brains are nothing more than hungry children that demand to be fed with entertainment and enlightenment. I'm not saying you must feel 150 percent motivated and "into" every single thing you're accountable for in your life. Some activities are simply less than stimulating. But there is a psychology behind having the right state of mind.

Think about it this way: In the creative field, there is an idea that the ability to create—whether it is a painting, a piece of poetry, a sculpture—is inspired by a muse. However, if the muse doesn't show up on command, a true creative can find a focus if they make an effort to explore within their craft. The same principle applies to casting off boredom. It also requires you to take the first step and break free from the shackles of monotony that have you in a chokehold.

When you make a conscious and eager effort to begin exploring your world, digging deeper, entertaining your brain, a force automatically lights up within you, and from then on there is a new excitement and energy about who you are. Since no one likes being around a boring person, this has the power to draw others to you. But to make this happen, you have to start searching. You can't expect the muse of curiosity to simply "be there." You have to go looking for it.

Here's a tip for implementing this advice immediately: Next time you are faced with some hum-drum task, change your inner dialogue. Don't allow the little voice in your head to ask, "Is this interesting?" Instead add one very important word that changes the entire context. Say, "*How* is this interesting?"

Always assume interest. It will change your life.

Start Asking Questions

There is a reason some journalists are great and others are simply "meh." The good ones thrive on their ability to be inquisitive about the world around them and ask questions. The words who, what, where, when, why, and how aren't just for reporters or journalists, however. They can be used by anyone, and they're definitely favored by curious people.

Consider children. Children absorb the world around them with an open mind driven by curiosity. A child's mind is constantly wondering about and exploring new things. After all, to a kid, most things are new! They ask how something works, why something is done a certain way, what something is, often to the chagrin of the adults who have to answer. Until, that is, one day the child stops asking. He or she becomes a grown-up and the sense of curiosity is stifled because there are bills to pay, clocks to punch and a to-do list to check off. Predetermined expectations begin to fog one's judgment.

What would happen to each of us if we never *stopped* asking questions? What would our lives look like? I believe the world would be a more accepting place, filled with people who don't recognize limits—and we would probably all be better for it. But the fact is, we *do* stop asking questions, and when we do we tend to grow old, boring, and stagnant.

When we don't have a routine to follow every day, it puts us at a disadvantage. But if you make a point to ask questions throughout your life, you will not only keep your brain entertained, you are more likely to discover new interests and envision possibilities you didn't know existed.

Curious people never take someone else's word for something. They ask the questions, dig deeper to get the details, and do their own detective work to satisfy their desire for discovery. Because they have the power to ask questions, they can discern the truth about who they are and what interests them.

Never Stop Learning

Curiosity inspires us to actively pursue knowledge. Every new awareness we encounter stimulates life, offering potential challenges and opportunities for growth. There has never been a better time in human history to dedicate ourselves to learning on a daily basis. We truly live in the age of information, a time when anything can be investigated and researched simply by pulling out a smartphone or opening an Internet browser! What a *wonderful* time to be a curious person!

Individuals who commit themselves to becoming lifelong learners have considerable power over people who simply coast through their days, adhering to the status quo or allowing the day-to-day grind to dictate who they are. Learners actively embrace new experiences as they seek information—and new experiences, no matter one's age, have the power to make life fresh and exciting. They stimulate your mind, free your internal energy, and liberate your thoughts. They provide an escape from the tension and stress that comes when your focus is on your work alone.

In all of this, however, it is imperative that you see the learning process as something that's fun. If you view learning as a burden, you will bury yourself even as you try to make positive life changes and it will defeat your purpose. Build the skills today that will benefit you in the future.

How Curiosity Will Help You in Your Career

I've spoken a lot in this chapter about why curiosity is important. I've placed much focus on the need to be inquisitive about things that happen outside of one's professional life. Curiosity helps develop a mindset that appreciates discovery; one that can empower and inspire you throughout life. It introduces you to interests that shape you. Most important for this discussion, it can benefit your career.

Curiosity will allow you to stand out to the people who matter throughout your career. Whether you are searching for a new job and want to make a great impression on a hiring manager, or if you are vying to be noticed by the folks in the executive office, your ability to show this characteristic is one of the things that will dictate whether you get noticed or passed over. It will show those who matter in your company and career that you are serious about your professional development. So volunteer to do something "extra." Attend a conference or continuing education seminar. Ask how you can advance in your company. Put yourself forward for a new opportunity. Such eagerness shows enthusiasm and engagement, and it displays your hunger to those around you.

My next point involves defining your core competencies as a professional and seeing where there might be "gaps." Core competencies are otherwise known as a skill set. Make it a priority to identify just what these are. Then, through your healthy sense of curiosity, improve and build upon them to ensure you're not simply "up to par" but setting the standard. Remember that in the professional world, skills and competencies change with the times. Recognizing this can ensure that you stay relevant, but also allow you to be realistic about what you are good at and where you need to improve.

Finally, a curious mind serves you well professionally when you need to step outside your comfort zone and think outside of the box. Those are well-worn clichés, but still a good description. Whether you feel nervous about attending a networking event or giving a presentation to a packed room, your curiosity will have instilled confidence in you and you'll show more flexibility and self -assurance than someone closed-off or afraid. You may discover a few weaknesses along with your strengths, but you will have the chance to truly realize your talent, potential, and drive.

CHAPTER 3

A Life Connected

As Kathy opened her office door for her final day of work, she was struck by the realization that it was the last morning she would enter her office eager to go about her business.

It's a weird feeling, she thought, taking in the space where she had spent significant time since her last promotion. *This place has been a second home of sorts.*

A wave of unexpected melancholy swept over her. She would miss her office. This private space had been *hers,* and she had definitely claimed it as such. Today, all of it would be packed in a box.

Shaking off the feeling, she strode to the other side of her desk and placed her briefcase on the surface in front of her. Going through the motions that she had done every morning for so long, she flipped on her computer. As she waited for it to boot up, she grabbed her iPhone from her purse and began scrolling through her email messages.

"Nothing pressing," she said under her breath, and then realized her folly. What could possibly be pressing? This was her last day!

With an uneasy smile, she placed her phone on her desk and sat back in her chair. Her desktop computer gave a familiar chime, signaling it was ready to go to work.

But on this last day, what was there to do?

"I suppose I can clean up my email," she said quietly, glad there were still things to check off her to-do list.

Kathy pulled up Outlook and settled into the familiarity of feeling connected. She had worked to ensure that her entire professional identity, all the contacts she had formed over the years, wouldn't be lost when she no longer had a "work email." She knew she wouldn't be staying in touch with everyone, nor did she really want to. But she had been proactive about making sure that people who did matter could still get in touch with her.

Her husband Bill thought she was crazy.

"Why do you still want to be tied to email? I thought you might be happy not having to check it every five minutes," he teased.

She wasn't going to check it every five minutes, she insisted. It wasn't about being tied to her iPhone. It was about staying connected, which to her was akin to having a relevant place in the world.

Bill had continued to press the issue.

"I think that's the *problem.* Being connected."

But though he had left it at that, his meaning suddenly struck her hard. Was she afraid of not being connected? Was she terrified of being "out of the loop"?

Uneasiness settled in her stomach. For years, she had been tied to her email, her voicemail, her Blackberry, and then to her iPhone. And with each improvement in technology, each development of some new device or time-saving app, her life had become more entwined with their invisible digital tentacles.

When was the last time she put down her phone and didn't glance at it for ten minutes? She couldn't remember. And that was only the tip of the tech iceberg. Starting tomorrow, she could begin to disentangle herself from this overreaching technology that had taken up residence in her life. Some people might feel liberated by that idea.

Kathy just felt anxious.

Where's the "Off" Switch?

As the elevator dinged and the doors opened, Kyle quickly straightened his shoulders. Stepping off, he almost collided with Jake, one of his direct reports.

The kid would have known he was there, Kyle thought ruefully, *if he didn't have his head buried in his damn phone.*

"Whoa there, Jake. Maybe you want to come up for air once in a while."

Kyle smiled at the younger man. His tone was half joking but also half serious.

Jake, a thirty-five-year-old fund manager, was always "on." There was no other way to describe him. Kyle had always liked the guy, even if he was a bit intense about the focus he placed on his job and future. You couldn't ask for a better employee. In Jake, Kyle saw himself, a worker who was willing to give it his all 24/7.

Personally, Kyle enjoyed seeing the time stamps on Jake's emails. It wasn't unusual for the guy to be shooting off emails at three a.m. He was like a 7-Eleven store, always open for business. And he was also about to assume Kyle's position.

The kid was his successor. Kyle's last day was Jake's first.

"Oh, man, hey Kyle. Sorry about that," Jake said distractedly. "I just got notification that the Carter Thomas account is moving forward. Finally." His face lit up briefly as another realization hit him. "But hey, what do you care? Today you put this place in the rearview mirror. *Bon Voyage.* Are you pumped?"

The question had caught Kyle off guard. A heartbeat before, his spirits had soared as Jake told him about the Carter Thomas account. His team had been after the account, worth $20 million to the firm, for a year and half, and here it comes . . . on his last day.

He couldn't deny his jealousy at that moment. He wouldn't be here to see its benefit to the firm. He wouldn't get to feel the satisfaction he always felt when a contract was signed, nor would he be around to manage the process, to handle the account implementation, witness the confirmation emails, and make sure everything went through smoothly and according to plan.

Deal with it, said a voice in his head that sounded surprisingly like his wife's.

"Carter Thomas," he murmured before realizing Jake was waiting for a response. "Oh yeah, excited. Definitely. Ready to get out of this rat race and have some fun." He smiled, not sure exactly what "fun" he meant.

"Well Kyle, that's great. Just know you are going to be missed. I have some really big shoes to fill and I can't thank you enough for everything you've done for me over the years. You taught me everything I know. I'm going to be burning the midnight oil just trying to make sure the guys on the top floor know they promoted the right person." He snorted. "I hope my wife doesn't mind."

Jake patted Kyle on the shoulder appreciatively and headed into the elevator, his head again buried in his device.

Tentatively, Kyle put a hand in his jacket pocket and extracted his own phone, noticing that he too had answered an email at two a.m. last night. His fingers immediately felt itchy. They wanted to check email, answer texts.

He felt guilty now for his thoughts about Jake. He hadn't always walked around the office with his head up. Being buried in tech toys wasn't just something Gen Xers and Millennials did. Kyle couldn't deny there was a direct correlation between who he was and the person Jake was on the verge of becoming. Swallowing hard, he tried to push away the thought that he'd not only ruined the kid's life but had created a monster.

CHAPTER 4

Cut the Cord

Once upon a time, you had to be right next to the phone if you were waiting for a call or had to make one. It was true in an individual's professional life as well as personal life. You had to be present to take the call.

Today, not so much.

You'd think that our access to technology, our ability to always be "on" would make us more productive and more efficient, and that might be true in some cases. But it's also fostered the growth of professionals who suffer from Attention Deficit Disorder. Rather than making our lives better, technology has made us more distracted, less productive, hyper-extended, and ultimately, less *present*. It has contributed to the quality of our lives and relationships by blending and blurring the lines between professional and personal, and it is costing us dearly in a variety of ways.

As we broach the topic of "cutting the cord" and whether technology impacts our ability to be successful, happy, balanced, and sane, consider these numbers, compiled on behalf of the Pew Research Internet Project (1). As of January 2014, the following figures hold true:

... Ninety percent of American adults have a cell phone;
... Fifty-eight percent of American adults have a smartphone;
... Thirty-two percent of American adults own an e-reader;
... Forty-two percent of American adults own a tablet computer.

When you consider how these devices are used, what do those numbers actually mean? The same Pew Research study notes that, "Sixty-seven percent of cell owners find themselves checking their phone for messages, alerts, or calls even when they don't notice their phone ringing or vibrating." The study went on to note that approximately forty-four percent of cell phone owners often keep their phone next to their bed when they are sleeping just to ensure that no text messages, calls, or other electronic updates are missed throughout the night (2).

If you're a person who thinks that sleeping with your phone next to your pillow is something that is "okay" or "just part of life," you may be a member of the twenty-nine percent who describe their cell phone as "something they can't imagine living without."

We are living in a culture of technological distraction.

Modern Technology: A Culture of Distraction

The modern workplace and the professionals who operate within it have become increasingly connected. As a result, we are less connected to ourselves and unable to find solitude and tranquility within our own minds. Today, meaningful encounters with the people around us are less likely to occur than they were a couple of decades ago.

According to a study by San Diego University, the average American citizen (and I'm not talking about the workaholics and high performers here) is bombarded with 100,500 words per day. They digest approximately twelve hours of information and media via technological sources day in and day out. That's half a day spent sending and receiving text messages and emails, leaving and accessing voicemails, handing out "likes" on Facebook, tweeting and retweeting, instagramming, "pinning," tagging and posting, as well as uploading, downloading, entering passwords, accessing files, Google Driving and Dropboxing, yada yada yada! Just considering that list makes me lightheaded and in need of a nap. It definitely appears we are all busy, but are we productive? There *is* a difference!

This culture of distraction is creating some troubling situations. As we become more disconnected from people and situations that actually exist in reality and more focused on the non-virtual world via the little device that lives in our pocket, we are unable to actually engage in thinking that requires creativity or analysis. We can't operate in a long-form context. Yet most of us want to be stimulated, entertained, and kept busy around the clock. This leads to anxiety, sadness, and worry when we try to power down or when our access to our technology devices is denied or prevented. (Why else do you think everyone on an airplane jumps to attention the moment it's wheels down? We can't wait to turn on our phones and find out what we missed during our flight!)

Though we seem to gain so much by having unlimited access to information and data around the clock, the fact is we are losing some very important things, as professionals and as people. Key ingredients to spur creativity and the ability to offer level-headed insight are threatened when we have no "gap" or downtime. Personal relationships suffer when we are not capable of focusing on who is across the table from us because we're too busy checking email or updating our Facebook status. By constantly "checking in" we are actually checking out.

The Death of Focus

We all remember the public service announcement where that actress says, "This is your brain," as she holds up an egg. Then, cracking it into a hot frying pan, she says, "And this is your brain on drugs. Any questions?" In my opinion, there should be a PSA that delivers the same message about our brains on technology. Rather than showing a fried egg, it could close with a haphazard and messy kitchen, the egg burning to a crisp after being left unattended on the stove because the chef was distracted with other things.

Our brains on technology have caused the death of focus. Scientists say that because we are now tasked not only with our day-to-day lives but also juggling email, phone calls, and other information, our behaviors have changed and our thinking patterns have morphed. These small bursts of information delivered *ad nauseam* around-the-clock have undermined our ability to finish a project or give undivided attention to someone in a meeting.

Moreover, science has also discovered that this ongoing and incoming ticker of information actually plays to primitive impulses hardwired in our brains. Think of it as a technological "flight or fight" response. We must immediately consider each bit of information and assess whether it is an opportunity or a threat, which in turn triggers dopamine. This causes a feeling of excitement to flood our brains and bodies, and it's addictive. When the data flood stops, we tend to feel bored, deflated, let down.

I have talked with and consulted some serious workaholics in my time. They are the sort of people who are always on, always going, completely addicted to the desire and need to push ahead, do more, work later, skip weekends. They thrive on constantly being busy, on continual stimulation, whether in the form of email, voicemail, or phone calls. Their work, and the functions that support it, make them feel alive. It's their drug.

This is Kyle in a nutshell. And when all of these forms of stimulation are taken away or no longer necessary, they feel empty, confused, despondent, and depressed. They feel like Kathy.

If Kyle thinks he can disconnect and go cold turkey after having lived most of his life in a constant state of being on, he is sadly mistaken. Even if he wanted to, his brain now has essentially been reprogrammed. Without the security blanket of his smartphone, he has no idea who he is.

Scientists have discovered that even after the technological and work-oriented multi-tasking ends, a lack of focus and the prevalence of disjointed thinking continues. Ultimately, once your brain has been programmed for a life on technology, there isn't a reset button for making it operate correctly when off technology.

And the results can truly be career-changing and health-threatening.

I recently heard a story about an individual, a man who was President of Business Development at a software company. We'll call him Tom Smith. Tom was in the middle of trying to close a $1.3 million deal to sell his start-up to a large organization. One day, the most important email of his career landed in his in-box: Confirmation that the deal would move forward. But guess what? Tom missed it. He overlooked it not just for a day or two, but for twelve days. Almost two weeks went by while the potential buyer wondered what the heck was going on. Why was it missed? Because Tom had two live computer screens on his desk that regularly pinged notifications about the delivery of new email to multiple email accounts, active instant messenger chats happening via three different platforms, a Web browser open to over ten different sites, a smartphone buzzing on the corner of his desk and oh, he was also trying to do his day-to-day work, writing computer code.

Though the deal was eventually salvaged, Tom said this experience probably won't inspire him to disconnect. He knows he's an addict.

Technological Quantity Equals
Lack of Real-Life Quality

We all know people with extensive LinkedIn networks and thousands of Facebook friends. But if you could peek inside their non-virtual life you would find them at home, by themselves, watching

TV (while simultaneously "living" on their smartphone)? Their phone isn't ringing off the hook with friends and loved ones calling, and they have nothing to do except go to bed at night and get up for work in the morning. Their lives and relationships are lived online. They barely exist in the non-virtual world.

How sad.

The irony of modern times is that we have extensive networks of "friends" and "partners" online. We know their comings and goings, we know their kids' names, and where they vacationed last summer. We are even aware of their political views, what they watch on TV at night, and know that they really love cat videos. And we acquired all of this information by spending no physical time with them.

Our ability to be more connected has made us less personal with those around us. Digital connections offer the illusion of companionship, but without the demands of a friend sitting across from you. And I doubt this will change anytime soon, especially as technology becomes even more pervasive in our culture. According to a Time Inc. study, half of all Americans say they prefer to communicate digitally rather than talk in person (3).

This is even impacting the most personal of relationships— those between married spouses and live-in partners. The Pew Research Center found that twenty-five percent of married or partnered adults who text have texted their partner when they were home together. At the same time, twenty-five percent of cell phone owners who are married or in a partnership have felt their spouse or partner was distracted by their cell phone when they were together. Eight percent of the same demographic said they have had an argument about the amount of time one of them was spending online.

The flip side? Nine percent of married or partnered couples have resolved an argument via text or in an online environment because they were experiencing difficulties resolving the issue face-to-face (4).

I'm not sure if that statistic makes me want to laugh or cry.

So what is the answer? Should we all simply turn off our phones after work? Is it necessary to banish technology so we have downtime and the chance to connect on a personal level with the people around us?

I would say yes. I believe it's essential to set technological boundaries, especially if you want your personal life to have meaning and if you value relationships with your spouse, partner, friends, clients, and co-workers. This is a teachable moment, one you should institute in your life right now. It's not about the "friend count" you have online. It's about the quality of the friends.

Would You Just Listen?

When was the last time you sat down with your spouse, a friend, or a co-worker, face-to-face, maintained eye contact, and just listened to what they had to say? How long could you sit there before you glanced at your phone? Ten minutes? Five? Thirty seconds? Or, let's consider the other person. How long before he or she picked up their phone?

Whoever gave in first, a powerful message was being sent: Something is going on somewhere else that's more interesting than what's being said here and the person saying it. Such an exercise definitely establishes what and who you care about.

During my presentations, I often ask audience members to grab a pen and paper and write the names of three people in their lives who are great listeners. You'd think three would be an easy number to reach, but it isn't. Listening is a skill that is being affected by the technology takeover, and as a society we are less able to gather our thoughts and express them. In turn, our shrinking attention spans prevent us from actually paying attention to the messages being conveyed to us verbally. Our communication skills are dying. And this isn't just about making sure you pay attention while your boss speaks in the boardroom. It's more important than that.

Being an effective listener helps you identify and understand the emotional undertones and implied messages delivered to you. It's something that technology doesn't allow. It is impossible to communicate effectively and empathetically via text message or in an email. Moreover, the importance of being a great listener has the ability to extend far beyond your professional life. Committing to listening improves self-esteem, maximizes productivity, and enhances personal relationships. You will even become a better public speaker. Listening is not a passive task. It is an active process and one that requires zero use of your smartphone.

Worker Burnout

High achievers are extremely driven people. If you are reading this book I'm sure you fall into that category. And while it's true that technology allows us to remain connected to our offices and work life, it also blurs the line between work time and downtime.

I recently spoke with a young woman who runs her own business. We'll call her Mary. She told me how proud she is of the Internet marketing company she has built and how she has created a high-functioning, albeit virtual, firm for herself and her workers. She even went so far as to say, "I can work from wherever I want, anywhere in the world."

This struck a chord with me and I pressed her on that idea. "Tell me how that works," I asked.

She proudly went on to say how she and her husband (who is also her business partner) had recently gone on a wonderful vacation across Italy and kept everything going back here in the States with her accounts and workers because she was connected the whole time.

"What type of vacation is that?" I asked.

She was suddenly speechless. She realized she was bragging that she was so connected that she had actually processed payroll for her employees and Skyped with her business manager on the train from Florence to Venice. She insisted she had a great time, which I am sure she did. But because she is the type that is always on, she is also incapable of turning it off, even for the sake of her mental health. And let's face it, no matter how committed you are to being the highest of the high performers, we all need some time off. Mary is no different.

Of course, if you're not self–employed like Mary, you may understand the value of time off, but, that doesn't make it easy to attain when your boss is emailing you after hours, or there is a pressing matter that demands your attention. No wonder some German firms such as Volkswagen, BMW, and Puma have instituted "email bans" in an effort to respect their workers' downtime. Managers have even been instructed to apply a principle of "minimum intervention" into workers' free time. At Volkswagen, the IT department turns off the email of some employees thirty minutes after their shift ends. BMW is planning rules that prevent workers from being contacted after hours. The goal is to reduce worker burnout and protect employees' mental health.

I believe these companies are on to something, and I wish more companies, including those in the United States, would follow suit. The bottom line? Successful people must be able to escape from work. If there was more focus on why workers shouldn't always be connected, we would be a happier and healthier society, and our companies would be more productive and profitable.

Of course, business and industry aren't the only ones to blame for the demands placed on workers. Our country just went through a major recession. Many jobs were lost, and for the people who remained employed, a sense of fear and worry became part of their day-to-day psyche. It's easy to understand why someone would over-commit. You want to prove your dedication and worth so you avoid the chopping block.

The amount of information and data a normal person is exposed to each day can be overload that contributes to burnout and company loss. According to Jonathan Spira, chief analyst at the New

York research firm, Basex, information overload cost American businesses just under $1 trillion in 2010 (5). When employees have to sift through needless emails and other electronic distractions, productivity suffers, which is expensive. And that includes the cost of turnover when a worker leaves in search of better working conditions and improved work/life balance.

A Center for American Progress study noted that the cost of turnover equals just over one-fifth of an employee's salary annually(6). This price tag goes up exponentially when the person who leaves is a high performer, manager, or supervisor.

Ultimately, it is in the interest of employers that employees can reliably switch off from their jobs, and it's to your advantage, as a high performer, to do so. Learn this lesson early. No one is immune to burnout. I guarantee your long-term success will be impacted if you don't begin changing such habits today. The most dangerous thing you can do as a professional with hopes, dreams, and goals is to drop into a mode of permanent activity. It cannot be sustained, no matter how much you try to.

Scattered Thoughts and Unoriginal Ideas

Information overload not only damages physical and mental health, it also cramps one's ability to operate effectively as a human being. Our dependence on technology has decreased our ability to manage thoughts and formulate sound ideas.

For instance, the act of simply reading for pleasure has dramatically declined in recent decades, though this very enjoyable hobby enhances thinking and engages the imagination. Reading a book helps your brain in way that visual media doesn't. As we spend more time with visual media and less with traditional print or other "antiquated" mediums, our ability to reflect, analyze, and think critically about the world around us is affected. While visual media allows us to process information better, there is more to thinking and understanding than simple data processing. The brain is an advanced piece of machinery, and if it isn't used properly it grows dusty and doesn't perform correctly. The more dependent we become on technology, the more we need it to actually tell us how to think and live.

We need some "blackout-inspired" creativity. Consider today's children. These little humans are supposedly fountains of creativity, the most imaginative and inspired life forms on the planet. But how many regularly and actively go on fantastic imaginary voyages anymore? How many sit down at craft time to make sculptures out of clay and Popsicle sticks? How many kids spend time outside devising their own games and building consensus amongst their friends as they make the leap to their next great adventure?

It hurts my heart that, for modern children, it is reality that's less enticing and exciting than what is found on their parents' iPads and smartphones. Their senses of wonder and mystery are being stifled and lost.

Certainly there are benefits to technology. These devices make certain things and tasks more convenient and pleasurable. But we have to be in charge of technology and not let technology be in charge of us. To achieve peak performance, we must commit to an environment that supports long-form concentration. To get in the zone—be fixed, calm, and present—we must place technology aside. It's not oxygen, not in your personal life or professional life. Don't treat it as such.

CHAPTER 5

The Power of Choice

Kathy heard a knock on her office door. Tearing her eyes away from her computer screen, she looked up to see who might be paying her a visit. It was Megan, one of the sales managers Kathy had groomed and mentored personally. Even with an age difference of about twenty years, the two women had gotten along from the moment Megan joined the company eight years ago. Megan had always been one of Kathy's favorites, and while she would never admit it aloud, she felt a fierce affection for the younger woman.

"Knock knock!" chimed Megan, popping her head in the door. "Who is ready for the day to end?"

Though Kathy had been dealing with a flood of emotions regarding her last day of work all morning, she tried not to grimace at Megan's words. With a smile, she rolled her eyes playfully.

"Oh stop. It's more likely that all of you can't wait to see me head out the door. *'Thank goodness she is finally retiring!'*"

Megan sat down on the other side of the desk. Crossing her legs, she waved a hand in Kathy's direction and snorted, "Are you kidding? I've been dreading this day for weeks, just knowing I'm not going to have you around anymore. We're all going to miss you like crazy. If I've told you once, I've told you a hundred times, I wouldn't be where I was today if you hadn't taken me under your wing."

Megan smiled and her face softened. Indeed, it looked like her eyes were starting to water, and Kathy knew Megan wasn't a crier. Especially in the office.

"I appreciate that, Megan. But chin up. I'll still be around. It's not like I am sailing into the horizon on a yacht." She wished.

"It won't be the same," Megan continued, and Kathy realized that her facial expression had changed subtly. Something about her young friend had hardened.

"I honestly don't know how I am going to put up with Susan."

The frown on Megan's face deepened.

"I just can't *stand* her. I can't believe they promoted her into your position. She's completely unequipped for the job. Someone needs to tell her that. I have dreams about being the one to do it."

Kathy sighed. She knew that Megan wasn't a fan of the woman who would be Kathy's successor. And Megan's vocal objection (at least behind closed doors) worried her. They worked in a highly politicized company, and Kathy knew Susan had the ability to make Megan's life miserable.

"I want to be honest with you, Megan. You need to watch it with Susan. She was passed up when I was promoted to this position and she has been itching to put her name on that office door ever since. I know she is a bit power hungry, but you need to play your cards right with her. I hope you aren't serious about butting heads. I think I trained you better than that."

Megan shrugged. "I don't know how long I'll last with her in charge."

"You probably will last much longer if you remember how to interact with her. You've come too far in this company to throw it away because you don't like someone. If you walk into her office on day one and tell her what's truly on your mind, remember that being a lion has consequences. You're too smart to play Russian roulette with your future career."

Megan sighed. "I know you're right. I suppose working under her will be an adjustment."

Nodding in agreement, Kathy considered how Megan had developed through their years together. Megan was much less reactionary than she had been years ago. Kathy was proud of the way she had become a methodological thinker and strategist. But she knew that sometimes the spitfire, no-holds-barred attitude still surfaced, and it had the ability to get her in trouble. Kathy wasn't against a strong woman speaking her mind so long as she thought about the words that were going to come out of her mouth before saying them.

"Megan, what have I told you every day since the day you started?" Kathy smiled. She knew that Megan had learned this lesson well and she was confident her mentee would carry it with her into the future.

"Make good choices," Megan said earnestly, looking at Kathy in admiration. "Don't worry Kathy, I know you're right. I won't let you down."

A Positive Brand

Kyle walked into the conference room to find his team already assembled. There was a nice lunch laid out and a cake. He knew they were doing a party after work, and realized his group was really milking a bit of downtime on his last day. But hey, after today he wouldn't have to worry about their productivity, so he decided to enjoy it.

"What's all this?" Kyle smiled, feigning surprise.

"Well, the party later is for everyone. We just wanted a last lunch with you," explained Trisha, one of his young recruits. "So surprise!"

Kyle laughed. "Jeez, guys, a 'last lunch.' I feel like I'm headed to the executioner."

Everyone dug into the food, and Kyle took a seat, enjoying the jovial spirit of his team. They were all young and hungry, and he had truly enjoyed leading them. There was little doubt in his mind that he would miss each of them in their own ways.

After some idle chit-chat and answering the question that he had been fielding all morning ("So Kyle, are you looking forward to a little R and R?" The answer again, "Absolutely!" The truth, "I have no idea what I'm going to do with myself."), the line of conversation changed.

"So how are we going to keep in touch with you Kyle? I suppose I can ask you if you're on Facebook now that you won't be my boss anymore," smiled Trisha.

Kyle snorted. Facebook. Social media. Time vampires that he was familiar with, but yet tried to avoid. Sure, he had a Facebook account, but he wasn't overly active. He had it primarily to see pictures of his grandkids that his own kids posted online. Truth be told, Kyle wasn't the biggest proponent of Facebook, not because he couldn't appreciate the social aspect of it, but because he found what people posted about themselves somewhat appalling.

Kyle was not, and never had been, an over-sharer. He had always had personal and professional boundaries, taught by his parents when he was young. He had been schooled on how to act in public situations, what was and was not appropriate behavior. He knew how to be thoughtful about the image and attitude he presented—his "brand" someone might call it—and felt it was an accurate assessment.

Kyle had always been responsible for his brand, which was probably why he had been so successful. He had never gotten drunk and loud at company cocktail parties. He had never been a gossip at work or in his personal life. He had made sure he was deliberate in his decision making. He was conscious of his internal dialogue before he opened up his mouth to speak, answering the questions, "Is what I am about to say appropriate? Is it valuable?" And he firmly believed that social media platforms broke too many of those rules. He couldn't believe some of the things that people offered up about themselves voluntarily.

"I'm on Facebook, Trisha," Kyle said honestly, "but I'm not really active."

"That's good Kyle," laughed Brett, a thirty-one year-old sales rep, "because you don't want to friend Trisha. All you hear about is her dating life and her love of wine. Not necessarily in that order. By the way Trisha, loved the picture that was posted of you from your high school spring break in Cancun. You know, the one of you passed out in the bathtub. Classic!"

A few of the guys tittered, and Kyle turned his attention to Trisha, who had flushed red in embarrassment.

"Seriously, Brett," she said sternly, "be quiet. That was 15 years ago." Trisha focused on eating. Kyle could tell she was working hard to avoid meeting his eyes. He knew his team members were friendly with each other. They often did happy hours after work and hung out in their downtime. But he also knew there had always been a barrier between them discussing their camaraderie in front of him. That line had been crossed today.

Kyle glanced at Brett, who had finished laughing and looked as if he was about to offer up more inappropriate information about his co-worker. The young man opened his mouth to speak but Kyle cut him off.

"That's enough, Brett," he said, trying to keep his tone light. He didn't like to be placed in the role of playground referee, and thankfully his team rarely required him to do so, but he also didn't want to suffer through Trisha's embarrassment. Her "brand" had taken enough of a beating for one day.

Wisely, Brett decided to change the subject and the team resumed their normal banter. The conversation remained on safe topics, but Kyle saw Trisha's mood had changed.

Lunch began to wrap up. People cleaned up and left the conference room. Kyle purposely lagged behind when he saw that Trisha had been left with the task of boxing up leftovers.

"Hey," said Kyle, approaching the young woman, "don't let an idiot like Brett get under your skin. Just ignore him."

Trisha frowned. "It's stupid. I should just unfriend him. He's such a troll. That picture was something one of my high school friends posted. I've told her not to tag me in stuff like that. She has no filter." Trisha paused. "Sorry, I don't know if you know how it works. Someone else can tag you in a photo and then . . ."

Kyle smiled. "I know how Facebook works. I may be older than you, but I'm not living in a time warp."

Trisha laughed. "Right. It's just sometimes I have to explain this stuff to my mom."

"No worries." Kyle considered his young worker and thought how valuable she had been to his team. She had a bright future if she played her cards right. "But in all seriousness, be careful what you put out there. The image you present to the world is your brand, your reputation."

"I know. I mean, Facebook is just personal stuff. It's not like I use it for professional networking or anything."

"That might be the case Trisha, but look what happened today. The personal crossed into the professional. I know Brett was just goofing around and I also know that you all are friends, but what if you run into a client somewhere and you aren't on your game? What if something from your personal life tarnishes your professional brand? Years ago, you could keep everything separate. You could put everything in tidy little compartments. But that's not the case anymore."

Trisha nodded and seemed to be thinking hard about what Kyle was saying. She cast her eyes down slightly and admitted, "You're probably right. I just hope you don't look on me badly after you heard what Brett said."

Kyle shook his head. "I do not. And I hope you don't think I'm lecturing you. You're a rising star, Trisha, and I would hate for anything to tarnish the brand you are building for yourself. Just keep that in mind when you put information out there."

She nodded her agreement and smiled. "Thanks Kyle."

His message complete, Kyle picked up some of the leftover lunch food and turned toward the door, ready to take it to the communal office kitchen for storage. Someone would eat it or take it home.

As he was about to leave the conference room, a final thought occurred to him and he turned back to Trisha.

"And for the record, remember to scrub your 'friends' list regularly. Never let someone else who isn't conscious of their own brand drag your brand down."

CHAPTER 6

Make Good Choices

There is a quote used by author Stephen R. Covey in the book *The 7 Habits of Highly Effective People: Powerful Lessons in Personal Change* that reads, "But until a person can say deeply and honestly, 'I am what I am today because of the choices I made yesterday,' that person cannot say, 'I choose otherwise'."

My inspiration for this chapter is not based on simply making good choices in your professional life, It's important in your personal life, too. As Kyle made abundantly clear, there has never before been a time when our personal and professional lives have the opportunity to co-mingle as they do today. The lines definitely are blurred, and the effect on someone's life of bad choices carries the ability to impact all sectors, with family and friends, work colleagues and clients. It's important to be vigilant every day in order to achieve long-term happiness, success, and overall peace of mind.

I have long adhered to the concept of "making good choices" in my own life. My son, who recently graduated from college and entered the "real world," was raised on those words. Every time we prepared to end a phone conversation, and each time he walked out the door, I would call after him: "Remember! Make good choices!" It got to the point where all I had to say was "Remember . . ." and he would finish the sentence for me. He might playfully roll his eyes now and then, and when he was a teenager I'm sure he thought I was nagging, but I am pleased to say that he has taken those words to heart. They are a part of him and who he has become as a young man. I have little doubt he will carry them with him throughout his life, no matter what he is facing. When he is at a crossroads and faced with a decision, they will be whispered in the back of his mind. He has grown to understand that the decisions he makes are important, and that whether his choices are good or bad, they have great power. The choices you make today will stay with you forever.

Use Your Brain . . . But Know Its Limitations

I have always been fascinated with the intricacies and landscape of the human brain. As wonderful as it is, however, it's important to realize that it's not always a rational place.

Think about it.

The genetic makeup of that organ, no matter how evolved we are as people and as a society, is the same as it was for humans who lived thousands of years ago. We may experience the same emotions, the same scattered memories, and the same lack of attention span as our distant ancestors. We also exhibit the same lack of decision-making ability and "fight or flight" responses. Our brains are not wired to automatically make the most "perfect" decisions.

A study by the Kavli Foundation related where neuroscientists examined brain activity during simple decision-making experiments (7). The scientists discovered that their subjects often had decided on a course of action ten seconds before they were consciously aware of having made any decision at all. The finding exposes a shortcoming present in our brains and leads to the worry, "If this is the case, how can we hope to make the right decisions?"

Do not fear. Knowing this is half the battle. It's by recognizing this weakness that we can increase our awareness about our choices.

A Choice to Make: Your Personal Brand

The word "brand" is bandied about a lot these days. Everyone is talking about brand management, not only for companies and organizations, but for individuals. And with good reason. Today's business world is more competitive than ever before, largely because of the Internet and the expansion of business into the virtual sphere. Professionals of all ages need to dedicate time and effort to strengthening their brand representation. This helps a person distinguish themselves. Defining and committing to a personal brand will make you unique if it's done well. It will help the people around you—clients, colleagues, friends, and loved ones—realize what you stand for. A personal brand should communicate your values and your ethics.

How does brand building contribute to your future happiness, success, and longevity? First, making the conscious decision to create and protect a personal brand will help you grow your network as a professional. Having a vast professional network is incredibly important to your success and will open up avenues and opportunities you probably never considered. When you develop a great network and combine it with a personal brand that communicates professionalism and poise, people will *want* to help you, connect with you, get to know you. When handled correctly, it will attract like-minded people like a magnet. But if you mismanage your personal brand, the opposite can happen, and send people running from you in droves.

Your personal brand involves the values you hold dear, but is also based on how you represent yourself, both online and in person. In the face-to-face arena, this means people judge you by your attitude, how you carry yourself, the words you use, and the consistency of the story you provide to the public. Your presentation skills and the clothes you wear are also part of your brand.

These concepts are also true in the online arena: What face are you presenting to the world? Are you constantly displaying pictures of yourself looking foolish? Do you argue with others, post ridiculous or offensive content, and use bad grammar when you make a status update on Facebook? Do you forget to use a filter or are you seemingly proud of the fact that you have #nofilter?

If you have answered yes to any of these questions, your personal brand might not be something to brag about.

I'm sure you have heard the old saying, "You only get one chance to make a great first impression." You need to understand this principle and realize that each and every day is a new opportunity to make another first impression with someone new. A new day is a chance to continue to strengthen your personal brand with the people you already know. This is true whether you are operating online or in person. You can't shut this off and you can't allow your personal brand to have downtime. It is who you are, and just like silver, if you ignore it, misuse it, forget to polish it, and set it aside, it will tarnish.

Check Your Attitude

Let's face it: A positive attitude will get you ahead, in a general sense, throughout your life. Some very specific attitudes will help you at work. Let's call them the five "E's": Enthusiastic, Efficient, Excellence, Early, and Easy.

An enthusiastic attitude is created by committing to being an eager participant in any project or task you are assigned. I'm not encouraging you to be a cheerleader. Critical, creative, and analytic thinking skills are still needed. I'm simply advising that you bring your energy to work with you. Yes, it's easy to feel sluggish on a Monday morning or after you have pulled some long hours. But if you commit to being interested in what you *do*, whether or not it's something you're really interested *in*, your work will be more stimulating and rewarding. It all gets back to the mindset you choose to have.

When deciding to be enthusiastic in your work, make sure not to throw proficiency out the window. Strive to be organized, on point, and continually competent. Your efforts will be noticed, especially by supervisors and project managers responsible for delivering a final product and need their team to get it done. Showing an efficient attitude will make you stand out when they need someone who can meet a deadline by taking the best route possible.

Next, it's time to pay attention to your 'tude by committing to excellence. Don't do it solely because your company's mission statement has that goal. Do it to make excellence part of your personal mantra. An attitude of excellence means pushing yourself harder, to show that you aren't content with good, that you want what you do to be *great*. When you dedicate yourself to excellence you work not only to meet expectations, but exceed them. With this commitment, you naturally exceed your peers, and get ahead.

The fourth "E" is "early." Early is not just a matter of timekeeping. It's an attitude you implement in your life. Think about when you are most productive. Is it when the phone is ringing, your email is pinging, and you have people constantly popping their heads into your cube or office? I'm betting the answer is no. My most productive times are when I get it into my head that I am going to get up or get somewhere early in order to prep and make sure I am ready for whatever task lies ahead. Being early allows you to organize your thoughts, identify what needs to be done, and get yourself in order. This in turn allows you to be enthusiastic about what is happening around you, improves efficiency, and contributes to your personal brand of excellence.

Finally, I want you to start thinking and being easy.

This doesn't mean being a doormat or a continual "yes" person. Having an easy attitude means that you aren't a complainer, a grumbler, or a nag. No one likes working with people like that. They make work and life unpleasant. When you're easy to get along with, talk to, and collaborate with, people will *like* working with you and you get ahead.

The lesson is this: Adopt a "Five E" attitude and become trusted, dependable, and influential. It helps you boost your credibility and burnish your brand, and the people around you will remember your name.

How Your Values Help You

Your values can define you and direct the choices you make, good and bad. How do they shape your choices and your life? First, identify and understand your values. Outline them as they relate to your work life and personal life. Doing this helps you realize your priorities and measure whether your life is shaping up as you'd like. Our values dictate the type of life we lead. When the way you act in public or private matches them, you're likely to feel happy, content, and satisfied. When there's a misalignment of values, you're likely to feel "off" or that you are operating in a state of "wrongness." You might not be able to put your finger on it, but a little voice inside your head is trying to tell you something.

Ultimately, personal and professional values exist for each of us, whether or not we make a conscious decision to recognize their influence. However, people who take the time to understand their importance are usually happier and more confident about their choices. Think about values as they relate to career goals. Say you really value your family time yet you're always at the office, plugging away and burning the midnight oil. If this is you, you're unlikely to feel excited about your career. You may also be incredibly stressed because the reality of your life is not matching up with your internal values.

Or what about this scenario? You don't consider yourself an overly competitive person but you are in a position such as sales, where you need to meet daily quotas. Your managers favor and reward high achievers, and you're expected to constantly be in

Accountability	Excellence	Perfection
Accuracy	Excitement	Piety
Achievement	Expertise	Positivity
Adventurousness	Exploration	Practicality
Altruism	Expressiveness	Preparedness
Ambition	Fairness	Professionalism
Assertiveness	Faith	Prudence
Balance	Family-	Quality-orientation
Boldness	orientedness	Reliability
Calmness	Fidelity	Resourcefulness
Carefulness	Focus	Restraint
Challenge	Freedom	Results-oriented
Cheerfulness	Fun	Rigor
Clear-mindedness	Generosity	Security
Commitment	Goodness	Self-actualization
Community	Grace	Self-reliance
Compassion	Growth	Sensitivity
Competitiveness	Happiness	Serenity
Consistency	Hard Work	Service
Contentment	Health	Shrewdness
Continuous Improvement	Helping Socie-	Simplicity
Contribution	ty	Soundness
Control	Holiness	Speed
Cooperation	Independence	Spontaneity
Correctness	Ingenuity	Stability
Courtesy	Inner Harmony	Strategic
Creativity	Inquisitiveness	Strength
Curiosity	Insightfulness	Structure
Decisiveness	Intelligence	Success
Democraticness	Intellectual	Support
Dependability	Status	Teamwork
Determination	Intuition	Temperance
Devoutness	Joy	Thankfulness
Diligence	Justice	Thoroughness
Discipline	Leadership	Thoughtfulness
Discretion	Legacy	Timeliness
Diversity	Love	Tolerance
Dynamism	Loyalty	Traditionalism
Economy	Making a dif-	Trustworthiness
Effectiveness	ference	Unity
Enjoyment	Mastery	Usefulness
Enthusiasm	Merit	Vision
Equality	Patriotism	Vitality

Hunter" mode. How likely is it you feel synergy at work or energized about what you do for a living?

Your values have the ability to direct your career path, but you have to know them in order to make educated and honest decisions about how to live your life. I suggest answering some of these questions when trying to determine your values:

... What are your most important *current* values? (i.e. money, family, career growth)
... What is your personal mission statement?
... How do you define happiness?
... What types of situations make you sad or stress you out?
... How do you feel about risk? Do you enjoy it or avoid it?
... Do you honor tradition? Or do you enjoy exploring new paths?
... How do you make yourself different from everyone else?
... What words do you relate with most?

Values are usually pretty constant, but they're not immutable. They can evolve over time based on what is happening in your life, so you should answer that list of questions from time to time. It is essential to stay in tune with your values in order to achieve balance and feel confident in the idea that you are making the best choices for you.

Listen to Your Instincts and Recognize Intuition

Let me begin with a caveat: Listen to your instincts and understand the value of intuition *but don't let them boss you around.* The brain is always working, compounding, and absorbing experiences that in turn get filed away in our long-term memory. That's where patterns begin to form and why, when something "feels" familiar, we instantly recognize it.

This is intuition.

Our instincts can be traced back to the first of our species. They fashion the way we respond to things. For our ancestors, this might have been their reaction when a hungry bear entered their camp, or when faced with a situation that threatened their survival. Although today we are programmed to respond in certain ways based also on our own life experiences, we are rarely faced with life and death situations, so snap decisions and instant responses aren't usually needed. It's only when we allow these things to power us that we take the ability to make a sound choice off the table.

Stay alert to the situation around you. Look for red flags when faced with a tough decision, but don't let the red flag blind you to whatever else is going on. To continually make choices that benefit your life, pay attention to detail. Consider the 360-degree view of your situation. Learn how to recognize how your body responds to stimuli such as stress, anger, anxiety, conflict, and confrontation since that might help you realize that extra attention to a problem or situation might be needed. Understand, though, that doing so requires you to develop special skills such as close observation, the ability to analyze carefully, critical thinking and reasoning skills, and most of all, good judgment.

It's one thing to listen to your gut and feel like you understand your instincts. It's another when you allow them to overpower your reasoning skills. As you consider a good choice or a bad one, work to combine your gut instincts with your ability to think logically and critically. The best decisions are made when these components work together. Make a habit of asking yourself a question in the moment of decision. Make your instinct, ability to analyze, and emotional IQ work in sync.

When faced with a situation where you are experiencing stress, anger or a burst of excitement, take a step back and postpone what is happening so you can return to a rational state. Once in that calm place, remember your original initiative or plan and determine if that plan aligns with the current situation or with what others around you are doing. This will help you see if your decision-making ability is being swayed or influenced by external pressures or if your thinking has been altered. Having this awareness can make the difference between effective decision-making and reactionary, knee-jerk impulses.

The best decision makers can "see around corners." They anticipate what is coming and can better prepare themselves for it.

Remember My Name

I believe that every driven, inspired, and motivated person wants to leave a legacy behind. I also think that part of good decision-making is based on understanding how people will view you and your decisions in the future. Are you building a personal brand that will be acclaimed? Or one of infamy?

Getting your peers, network, friends, colleagues, and managers to remember your name and think kindly of you requires personal brand building. And remember that it's an ongoing process. It won't happen overnight.

When we hone the ability to make good choices, we get to know ourselves better. Making good choices in one's professional and personal life and realizing how closely these two worlds are aligned will make you more conscientious, poised, polished, and mindful. There will be fewer moments when you wake up worrying about a choice or about what someone thinks of you because you have the confidence that you have done right.

Following the advice in this chapter will make your personal brand unique, attractive, and irresistible, whether you are making a presentation to a packed auditorium or hanging out with your friends. You will feel confident about the choices you are making and the life you are leading. You will be a magnet for positive energy, professional opportunity, and personal happiness. And those around you will remember your name.

CHAPTER 7

Continuity of Culture

Kathy couldn't believe the day was almost over. Her load had not been heavy since it was her last day, but the weight of her heart had been more than enough to bear. She was both elated and fretful. How strange that all of her life she had managed change on the job and was now struggling as she faced her own change.

She felt as if she had been saying good-bye all day.

"What I need is that glass of champagne that is sure to await me at the party," she said to herself, smiling and glancing at the clock, knowing it was almost time to head downtown to the venue where the party would be held.

Kathy got up from her desk and walked out of her office to where her administrator, Pete, sat.

"Hey Pete, I was wondering if you could call down to building maintenance and see if they might have a hand truck I could borrow briefly to get some of these boxes to my car."

Kathy wasn't afraid of some heavy lifting, but hoped to make the trek in as few of trips as possible.

"No worries Kathy. You shouldn't have to do manual labor on your last day. Besides, why else do I go to the gym?" Pete smiled.

"Show me the boxes and give me the keys to your car. I'll handle it."

Thanking him, Kathy gave some instructions and Pete set off. At the same moment, Susan—her successor and the woman Megan had worried about earlier in the day—rounded the corner of the hallway and called a greeting, "Kathy! Just the woman I was looking for! Do you have a few moments to spare? I have some issues to discuss while I have you here."

Kathy nodded cordially. It was just like Susan to wait until the closing minutes of a day to bring up issues that could have been addressed earlier on.

"Of course. Come into my office, or should I say *your* office?" Kathy teased, noticing that Susan didn't wait for her but led the way. Kathy decided to let it go, unless she sat down behind the desk. Thankfully, Susan didn't.

Once the two women were situated, Kathy took charge of the conversation. "So what can I do for you, Susan?"

"Well, let me get right to the point, Kathy. I've already started planning, at length, for the role I am going to assume starting tomorrow. Of course, I know it will no longer be your concern, but I plan on making some significant changes. I think some things can be done better."

Kathy tried not to grimace. Susan wasn't one to mince words. At all. And while it's true that it wasn't something that Kathy needed to be worried about, she did worry for her team. Kathy had had a hand in developing a great many people, not just Megan. She had been committed to their work as a team as well as to each individually.

"I understand. And that is your right, of course. How can I help you?"

Kathy decided to probe more. She needed to find out if Susan was actually looking for help or advice, or if she was simply eager to start throwing her weight around and wanted Kathy to know she was redundant.

"Obviously," Megan said, "you have been successful in this role, and everyone appreciates what you have done, myself included."

Kathy nodded appreciatively while staying aware of the fact that she was being "buttered up."

"I'm going to start with a team assessment right off the bat. I really think I have to restructure the roles of some people in this department. I think I am also going to have to address some productivity vampires."

Kathy's eyes shot up at the word choice. "Productivity vampires?"

Susan nodded. "Yes, like the end-of-the-month team lunches. They last way too long and nothing ever gets accomplished. I think it encourages too much wasteful spending and eats up too much of the day."

Kathy felt like rolling her eyes and defending the lunch that they had been doing for the past few years. Her team had continually come in under budget, and she used the extra padding in her expenses for a regular treat where they could get together off-site and commune as a group. The team lunch had been noted as something the group really appreciated and enjoyed, an added "benefit" of the job without being over the top. And plenty had been accomplished at those lunches. The environment alone allowed the team to regroup, celebrate their monthly accomplishments, and create a place where new ideas could be presented and discussed.

Susan wanted to begin her new role by cutting something that had benefited the team and the culture of their department.

No wonder Megan is worried, Kathy thought. How could she get Susan to think differently?

"Hmm, I see," said Kathy, thoughtfully. "And how do you plan on telling the team about this change? I'm sure you've thought about it at length, eliminating something that's been a tradition for so long."

Susan looked at her blankly and shrugged. "I figure I'll just tell them. They have to understand that some things are going to change. Beside, those are dollars that could be better spent elsewhere. You have to think about the bottom line." Susan met Kathy's eyes. "I mean, I know I don't have to tell *you* that," she said, her words dripping with meaning, "but you and I just have different styles."

"Indeed," said Kathy. "So let me ask you then, what traditions, what part of our departmental culture, are important to you? How do you plan to inspire and energize everyone? I found that our monthly lunches were very good at accomplishing that goal. It gave everyone something to look forward to, especially since the morning of the lunch is when monthly sales numbers are posted. And we have been consistently successful, but I don't have to tell *you* that," Kathy smiled sweetly. "How do you plan on continuing that success and getting your team motivated if you start playing the take-away game on day one?"

Susan waited a moment and seemed to consider this. Her brow furrowed. She looked like she hadn't truly considered the *why* for the monthly lunches, how that reward system appealed to her future direct reports.

"Maybe we can do something different," Susan said weakly, "like hand out awards or plaques for top performers."

Kathy sighed. If Susan had been paying attention at all or taken the time to review the recent performance reviews of individual team members, she would have discovered that the group was more motivated when participating in a collaborative setting. Indeed, that's how they had been consistently successful. Susan wanted to manage them in a way that was at odds with the key performance drivers.

Kathy decided to advise Susan right then and there.

"Susan, please understand I am not looking to tell you how to do your job. I believe that once you 'get your feet wet' so to speak, you will learn what this role requires of you. Maybe then you and the team will develop new ways to work together and you all can make changes based on those discussions. In the meantime, I advise against taking things away from a group of people who work exceptionally well together. They will be dealing with a lot of change in the coming weeks. I know they are willing to work *with* you, but they also have to have continuity in the culture they have grown *accustomed* to. Don't take away perks and traditions that are so engrained in their minds and tied directly to how they perform, individually and collaboratively. I believe you will find them much more responsive to your management style if you are accepting of the cultural architecture that has been built around here."

Susan nodded and smiled, and a new softness found its way onto her face.

"I think you're right Kathy. Maybe I was being too aggressive. Thank you. I obviously have some big shoes to fill."

Kathy felt genuinely appreciative of the compliment and thanked her.

Getting up to leave, Susan headed toward the door, then stopped and turned back to smile. "I know I'll see you at the party tonight, but I don't want to forget to ask this. Do you mind if I keep your number in my phone and give you a call? I hate to bother you, but I think I might have some questions."

Kathy laughed. "Of course. Call me anytime."

She felt immediately more confident that maybe, just maybe, Susan, and her team, would be all right.

Architect for Change

Kyle was about to call it a day. There was a party waiting for him a cab ride away, and he knew his wife Maggie had a new dress for the occasion. He didn't want to keep her waiting.

It had been a good day, and as he looked around his office, he realized he felt okay. Retirement was going to be an adjustment, but it was going to be a challenge he would tackle head on. He had been successful throughout his life. There was no reason to think he was going to crash and burn now.

He said a silent good-bye to the place where he had spent many hours and closed the door behind him, only to find Jake in the hallway.

"I hope you are leaving the place nice for me," Jake said, motioning toward the office. Kyle chuckled. No doubt Jake was already thinking about how he would rearrange the furniture.

"Let's just say I haven't left any booby traps behind. Are you on your way to the party?"

"You bet. Want to share a cab?"

The two men agreed. Kyle didn't mind the company. It would keep him from focusing too much on the enormity of his own situation.

Once in the cab, Kyle pointed the conversation to Jake. He was frankly tired of talking about retirement.

"So you all set for tomorrow then? Moving into the office first thing?"

Jake shrugged and pulled out his phone, his attention focused on the screen. "Yeah, probably not tomorrow, but next week for sure. I haven't called a meeting with everyone until Monday morning. I actually think we are going to start doing some virtual work, focus more on working remotely and see how that pans out. The commute is just not worth it anymore. Need to shake things up. All of us are always connected anyhow. Not like I need to see everyone in person. I actually think it's better if I *don't* see some people at all." Jake smirked.

Kyle nodded. A virtual workplace. That was the sort of thing guys like Jake thrived on. They were connected, but they weren't. Kyle wasn't sure how that would go over in this office. The top guys in the C-suite were very old school. He wasn't sure Jake was fully aware of that.

"Well, buddy, it's your call now. But remember, I've said it before, you need to come up for air from that thing occasionally," said

Kyle, pointing at Jake's phone. "There is a culture at that office, and the guys in charge like face time. And no, I'm not talking about the Face Time app. They're going to need to see you and they're going to need to see you *with* your team."

"But we can save a ton of costs, and I mean, guys my age, no offense, we are just better when we are online."

Kyle nodded and thought about this statement. Some of the people he had been responsible for grooming and managing were incredibly productive with their phones in hand. But there was an established culture at the firm. Absent usually was interpreted as "not working."

"I understand, Jake. And I'm not trying to step on your toes here. I think you are in a unique position, and times are changing. Just remember to consider the existing company architecture before you start knocking down walls. You want to make sure you have a blueprint that works with the foundation that is already in place. Maybe start with baby steps when it comes to introducing new processes or work styles. The guys up top are going to be more accommodating when change is gradual. You might also want to try introducing it in such a way where the executives think it was their idea. Seemed to work in the past. Or so I have found."

Jake slid his phone into his jacket pocket and looked at Kyle thoughtfully.

"You know boss, you might be on to something." The cab pulled up in front of the steakhouse where the party was being held. "I got the fare," said Jake, swiping his corporate AMEX. "Remember I'm the one with the expense account still," he smirked. "Come on. I think I need to take advantage of the next couple of hours and pick your brain while I have the chance. You might know more than I realize."

Kyle slid out of the cab's backseat feeling good about the advice he could provide to his successor. "You got it kid. Now come on and buy me a drink."

CHAPTER 8

Traditions Maintained

Tradition can be both fragile and dynamic. Some traditions allow for the illusion of permanence and continuity to be achieved while touching us, connecting us, and expanding us as people and collaborative groups. They are legacy-building and should be considered as part of the foundation for any leader's successful and remembered career. And while you might think traditions only exist in the realm of family holiday get-togethers and annual events in our personal lives, maintaining traditions at work is important to achieving happiness, satisfaction, and long-term success.

Customs contain valuable knowledge collected over time. They thrust us into the position of "cultural architect," creating the groundwork that allows us to retain our balance while growing and developing as professionals. In challenging environments like the modern workplace, traditions should be considered the anchors that keep us moored and steady amidst the waves of constantly changing seas. Workplace traditions connect us to the past, and as long as we don't dwell there too long, can instruct us on useful elements that aid in future success.

Tradition needs to be respected and honored to craft a career path to be proud of in the future. It will help you be remembered after you pass through the organization's doors as an esteemed veteran.

What is Tradition in the Workplace?

Our personal lives are chock full of traditions. We salivate as we think of Thanksgiving dinner, honor Opening Day at the ballpark, and can't wait to drink a green beer and toast St. Paddy. There are also traditions in the workplace that impact our professional lives. They are keys to the establishment and continuity of company culture and instrumental in job satisfaction. When you check the dictionary for definitions of "tradition" and "culture," you will find them very similar.

Tradition is defined as "the transmission of customs or beliefs from generation to generation." Culture means "the sum of attitudes, customers, and beliefs that distinguishes one group of people from another." Tradition is the establishment of a practice and culture that develops when that practice is sustained and respected.

Traditions in the workplace come in the form of activities that build relationships and strengthen bonds between team members. They boost morale and create a sense of energy both inside and outside the office. The best workplace traditions are those that are highly anticipated and talked about for long periods of time before and after they occur. They create a legacy for the company and its workers alike.

What's more is that workplace traditions, while they might involve an annual retreat or even an exotic trip for high performers, do not have to be costly or a drain on resources. They can be something as simple as a team lunch or a "Casual Friday" at the office. Such things can be more important to overall culture and morale than many people might believe.

Cultural Continuity Allows for Increased Engagement

Workplace traditions are a key element in the creation of company culture and the construction of positive morale. When continuity of traditions is present, the results encourage increased employee motivation and long-term job satisfaction. Traditions are activities and events that cannot be forced. They are established over time. Leaders must provide continuity in annual messaging about honoring traditions. If not, the "tradition" becomes mainly a blip on the calendar, lacking importance. People get away from it, leaving a feeling of disconnect permeating an organization and a team. It ends up contributing to a decrease in employee engagement.

A Gallup poll released at the end of 2014 noted that less than one-third of all U.S. workers felt engaged in their jobs. About fifty-one percent said they were not engaged and 17.5 percent stated they were actively *disengaged* at work (8). Gallup defines engagement as when employees are "involved in, enthusiastic about, and committed to their work and workplace" and notes that this is a key indicator in predicting organizational performance outcomes.

This research also found that younger workers are the least engaged with their positions. Typically they are the individuals at the lowest levels of the organization. Conversely, managers and leadership executives had the highest levels of engagement. Unfortunately, it is this mix that often leads to the "employee engagement issue" being turned into an item on the human resource department's to-do list, and not considered a strategic initiative that drives accomplishment, inspires continuous improvement, and spurs performance. Engagement is the reason people feel happy with their profession. They are driven to do more, show commitment to their careers, and make the conscious decision to be involved in their day-to-day life and not just a worker bee. It is absolutely key to crafting a meaningful life.

At the same time, many people in leadership positions are unaware that workplace traditions influence employees' behavior—for good when handled correctly, and the opposite when managed recklessly. Traditions should be celebrated to motivate individuals and teams. They remind people about collective goals and how these unique rituals define and provide continuity to an organization's culture.

Finally, a leader who wants to be remembered long past retirement must accept that the organization's traditions are key to success and discard the notion they simply perpetuate the status quo.

Feeling Connected to Work

We live in a professional world where the message is always to go faster, harder, and longer. Get more done, accomplish more, think more, do more, more, more, more! Technology further complicates this "do more" working environment, and as I discussed in a previous chapter, the fact that we are always connected, perpetually on, means we feel disconnected from people and activities around us. There is a divide that has developed in our lives, personally and professionally. Although we are always tied to our work by countless electronic tethers, we are actually more disconnected as living, breathing human beings. Add that many people today work remotely, and it's even more necessary to find a way to connect within an organization.

A recent study completed by Dr. Gregory Walton, a Stanford University professor, and published in the *Journal of Personality and Social Psychology* studied the circumstances related to working hard (9). Does this happen in a more positive way when people feel connected to others? Or when working alone?

It's a knee-jerk reaction to think that working alone means you will be more focused or productive and more capable of attaining professional goals. The study actually found that when people feel they are working with others to reach a goal, they are more motivated and eager to pursue the achievement, even when there's no extrinsic reward such as a raise or bonus. The rule here is that people will work harder and more cohesively when there is a feeling of connection. And it is here where workplace traditions come in.

Traditions have the power to connect us and help us feel more fulfilled. The feeling of being connected to other people, to a mission or goal, helps promote happiness, both in the short- and long-term. A study conducted at Purdue University shows that feeling connected can literally add years to your life.

I recently consulted with a new manager who was assuming a leadership role. She believed the best strategy she could immediately employ would be to do away with the traditions put in place by her predecessor. She felt that these practices and principles were the remnants of a different management style and wanted to implement new traditions that established herself as the emerging leader. It was not her intention to be hard-handed in this approach, but she quickly found that her team was taken aback by the idea, and felt they were being punished. The employees rejected a leadership style that impacted the budding relationships she was working to develop with them. It wasn't until she understood that the traditions were something the team appreciated and felt aided in connecting them to their jobs that she realized she made a huge mistake.

This individual's mistake is an easy one to make, and I told her that. One of the most important things a professional needs to realize, whether if they are the person in charge or a non-management employee, is that work is a social thing and should be treated as such. I don't advocate treating your work life like every day is a party, but to remember that the act of work is not something that a person does alone. It is an activity done *with* people *for* people.

This might be a hard concept to accept, especially if you are a leader with a job to do and deadlines to meet. Feeling confusion about these two areas creates a sense of professional misalign-ment. If you can't connect with the people you spend so much time with, loneliness and a sense of isolation settle in and your job sat-isfaction and overall happiness suffer.

The rule here? Don't underestimate the value of tradition and connectedness. People need something to count on, and today's workplace doesn't always offer that. Encourage traditions that connect people rather than those that separate and divide.

Changing and Rehabilitating Traditions

Workplace traditions don't simply promote togetherness and har-mony within a professional setting. They should be implemented as a method for obtaining results. Traditions can morph and change over time to get improved outcomes from an activity. Of course, this should be tested to see if it is successful.

I'll give you a for instance from my personal life.

A few years ago, my family got together and decided that in-stead of doing the traditional Thanksgiving spread—turkey, stuff-ing, the works—we would do an Italian Thanksgiving . Now, I love Italian food. But at the end of the meal, although we were full on carb-heavy comfort food and happy spending time with each oth-er, an odd feeling had settled over our communal table.

Something just felt off.

We had messed with a tradition that didn't need changing, and it had modified the overall feeling of the day. It was Thanksgiving, but it didn't *feel* like Thanksgiving. Memories of loved ones passed, and tastes and smells we associated with good times of yesteryear, were gone. We had created a void where one hadn't existed. We had to plan another dinner a week later to make sure the time-honored traditions were properly handled. We might have gotten an extra day to spend together as a family because of this experiment, but it also taught us a valuable lesson.

Don't mess with a tradition that isn't broken.

On the other hand, traditions sometimes need tweaking. When you feel the, "We have to do it this way because we always have" syndrome, it might be time to stop and re-evaluate that tradition. You might feel this way at work if the makeup of a team has changed or the company has morphed its mission to keep pace with an evolving marketplace. In that situation, it's okay to put a new "twist" on a workplace tradition, especially if the old way isn't working. If you don't want to eliminate it completely, develop a mindset of being open to change. Be flexible and ask your colleagues and team for their ideas on how to make it better.

At the end of the day, if there is a consensus that people feel they are being forced to do things they don't want to do, or if the tradition gets in the way of making progress, the best course of action might be to disband it and develop a new tradition your team can get behind.

Implementing Traditions at Your Office

Traditions should play an important part in your career, and it's never too late to start one in your office. Your mindset must be one that doesn't consider a tradition an "activity" but one that allows you to learn about your co-workers, build a team, facilitate an aura of excitement and energy, and create a community. Your job as a leader is to serve as the architect of a culture. You must demonstrate the values you promote to your team and ensure they are integrated on a day-to-day basis. This is how you build consensus and gain respect.

Many readers may not yet be in positions of career power or responsibility, but it's possible to start establishing traditions during an early authority role. We all know leaders who command respect and exhibit charisma. They are the individuals people *want* to work for because they value direct reports and inspire loyalty. Since some of the best workplace traditions emerge naturally, here are some ideas you may want to incorporate with your team:

... Celebrate holidays together while remembering to be aware and considerate of other cultures, religions, and ethnic groups.

... Bring employees together on a quarterly basis for team building.

... Create a tradition that is used when on-boarding a new employee or team member.

... Establish a tradition for recognizing staff anniversaries and birthdays.

... Do something that commemorates the founding date of your organization.

... Develop a monthly or quarterly recognition or rewards practice.

... Brainstorm and implement a weekly tradition, something that makes the day-to-day fun such as bring-a-pet-to-work day, Casual Friday, or a weekly breakfast or lunch.

... Host an annual event or celebration, such as a banquet at a nice restaurant, a staff retreat, or other highly anticipated outing.

Traditions establish organizational legacies and are the key to a great culture. The benefits that accrue will be worth it. Traditions will:

... Create something timeless to hold onto, honor, and continue.

... Build meaningful connections between employees and your organization or team.

... Allow for the development of a shared history, rich with stories and experiences.

... Bring people together, forge bonds, and foster a sense of belonging.

... Strengthen the identity of an organization.

... Inject energy into the workplace, heighten moral, and create a positive work environment.

Final Thoughts on Tradition at Your Workplace

Beginning a workplace tradition won't happen overnight. Like any long-term task, it should be worked toward, strategized on, and developed. Don't underestimate the value of tradition. Realize it will give your employees or team members a feeling of connection to their careers and company. Remember it is not your responsibility as a leader to decide which traditions may be important to the people around you, and which ones won't. Ask, listen, and observe. Get a sense of what the team values and what could be retired or changed.

Establishing, sustaining, and honoring tradition can reap considerable rewards for an organization while leaving a valuable mark that endures beyond your physical tenure. Start a new practice that fortifies the connections among people, and between people and their work. Don't force it, but if the practice fills a need, it could become a tradition and one of your most important career legacies.

CHAPTER 9

Good-Bye

Kathy knew the party was winding down. Looking out across the floor of the dining room, she picked out a few familiar faces—some younger people from her department who were probably considering their next stop after this and a few veterans who looked like they were dedicated to the idea of having a nightcap before heading out. She smiled, it had been a great party—made ever more memorable because her family had also been able to make it.

"Here you go Mom, I think you deserve one last glass of champagne," said Lindsay, her oldest daughter, placing a flute of bubbly on the table in front of her.

"I honestly think that I have had enough," laughed Kathy, even while she took a small sip of the pale gold liquid.

"Ah, lighten up, you can sleep it off tomorrow," said her daughter.

Kathy raised her glass. "I will certainly offer cheers to that."

The two women sat in silence for a moment before Lindsay spoke.

"Are you sad? That it's all over I mean?"

Indeed, Kathy had been battling that question all day—and even now, she wasn't sure.

"I don't think that *sad* is the right word for it. Melancholy, excited, ready, hesitant. My feelings are contradictory at best."

Lindsay nodded kindly at her mother. "You should be proud of yourself Mom, truly. You've had a wonderful career. And if it wasn't for women like you—and all you went through to climb the ladder, break barriers, achieve success—I don't know if I would have the career that I have today."

Kathy felt tears prickling the back of her eyes. She had promised herself all day that she would not cry—and here her daughter was, getting the best of her.

"Oh stop," shushed Kathy with a smile.

"No Mom," said Lindsay earnestly. "You have a great story, you've had an amazing journey. You started off as a secretary at this company after all! And look at where you are now. Executive Vice President. And I'll never forget what you taught me from the time I was little—that I could be whatever I wanted to be as long as I kept an open mind, didn't put limitations on myself, and always remained open to change. I remember you saying that I should never get too comfortable and that reinvention is simply a part of life. You taught me that I should explore whatever interests happened to pop onto my radar and that above all else, I should always remain authentic and true to myself. I've carried that with me, because I know that you built a career on those beliefs and I figure that if I really took those lessons to heart—well, I might not turn out so bad myself."

Kathy worked to swallow the lump that had been building in her throat. There was no denying that she was proud of Lindsay—the young woman would probably make partner at her law firm within the next year or two—not bad for a thirty-four-year-old. Indeed, she was proud of all of her kids—all driven to succeed, focused on doing their best—she and her husband had worked hard to instill those values in them. And apparently that effort had paid off.

"Thank you Lindsay," said Kathy quietly.

"No," smiled her daughter. "Thank you Mom."

Taking a deep breath, Kathy felt a sense of calm suddenly wash over her. For the first time that day, she felt the mess of emotions that had been bouncing around her body ease their grip. The jittery feeling that had been flooding her heart subsided.

Kathy smiled as the realization hit her.

She was ready.

It was time for the next chapter of her life to start.

"Come on Lindsay. I'm ready to go."

And her daughter nodded at the words as both women rose from their seats.

"Of course you are."

Hello

Kyle made one final lap of the restaurant—saying his good-byes. Even though he felt as if he had been saying the words all day, he knew this time it was for real.

It had been a good night, a positive final day—actually, it had been a great career. And he realized that as he shook hands, accepted hugs, and said his closing words to the people who were now his former colleagues, that he was happy. Hell, he was *excited* even.

Joining his wife Maggie, who was holding her coat and chatting to a woman who worked in the human resources department, Kyle realized that he was fine, that he was ready to go. He had done all he could do. He had been successful. And now it was time for what is next.

Whatever that may be.

It's true that he had been so focused on building his professional legacy since the first day on the job. And in retrospect he knew that maybe he could have done some things differently along the way.

But there was no sense worrying about the shoulda's and woulda's at this point—it was about what he was going to do with tomorrow.

Helping Maggie on with her coat, Kyle took a final glance back at Jake, his successor, and secretly hoped that he had gotten through to the kid. Jake had the opportunity, from this day on, to do everything that Kyle had done—and he had the chance to do more and have a richer experience if he ended up taking Kyle's advice and finding the balance that Kyle didn't always have. Catching the younger man's eye, Kyle threw him a thumb's up and a smile as Jake raised his glass to him from across the room.

The world is your oyster kid, thought Kyle, a smirk on his face.

"What's that look for?" Maggie asked with a smile as she regarded her husband.

Shaking his head and shrugging, "Ah, nothing. Just thinking back. Been doing that all day."

"You ready to go?"

With conviction in his voice and an affirmative head bob, Kyle offered his wife his arm.

"You know what? Yes. I. Am."

Exiting the restaurant, Maggie pointed the way to where she had parked the car earlier upon her arrival, but Kyle pulled her back, encircling her with his arms.

"Are you in a hurry to get home?"

Maggie's face took on an inquisitive look. "Why?" she smiled. "What are you thinking?"

Kyle kissed her nose and looked down at his wife's lovely features. He appreciated her so much—and he didn't think he told her that enough. Maggie had been with him through thick and thin, richer and poorer, and maybe he had not always been as attentive as he could have been.

Here was his shot. He had evolved and changed throughout his professional life—and now it was time to reinvent the personal side of his existence.

"Well, it's just that the night is young, and you have that beautiful dress on, and we're out in one of the best cities in the world, and I was just thinking...how about a little dancing?"

Maggie let out a playful snort and smacked his shoulder lightly, even as he continued to hold her close.

"Dancing? Right. You've never wanted to go dancing before."

Kyle looked at her seriously. "I know. And that's all going to change. You're looking at an old dog who has decided he wants to learn some new tricks."

Maggie considered her husband. "You're serious, aren't you?"

"As serious as a heart attack, which just as a side note, is something that I hope to avoid in retirement." Kyle squeezed Maggie ever so slightly. "Come on. It'll be fun and we've got nothin' but time."

Maggie smiled broadly. "I think I might like the way retirement looks on you."

Kyle let out a laugh and released Maggie from his embrace, grabbing her hand and deciding to lead the way. He knew of a club just a few blocks away that would be right up Maggie's alley. It was a place where they could do the twist and pretend they were in college—a throwback club that specialized in making all of that which is old new again.

Kind of like him.

"And while we are walking, start thinking about what you want to do tomorrow."

Maggie laughed gleefully and Kyle's heart soared.

He had nothing to be afraid of. This was just the next step—and it was time to meet the next new version of himself.

CHAPTER 10

Reinvention

Throughout my life, I have had a passion for reinventing and reimagining myself. C.S. Lewis said, "You're never too old to set another goal or dream a new dream," and that is what reinvention is—change. Sometimes, we don't expect reinvention to come our way. But leaving a job or a relationship, deciding to move for a new opportunity, being presented with an alternate form of thinking—these situations offer an opportunity to take control of who we are and want to become. If we ignore the likelihood of reinvention based on circumstances that seem beyond our control, we risk never reaching our full potential.

Reinvention isn't just a professional possibility. Be open to personal reinvention too. Wherever you're starting from, you will evolve through the people you meet, the events you experience and the level of risk you embrace. All contribute to who you are and what you become. Believing in this concept will make you a richer, more knowledgeable, and savvy person. Reinvention keeps you relevant.

Reinventing oneself offers the chance of a different future. Your past is just that. Be the very best version of yourself by cultivating all parts of you and making a commitment to personal authenticity. Be the professional, the traveler, the reader, the artist, the lover, the adventurer, the spouse, the parent, the writer, the friend, the (fill in the blank). You are not one dimensional!

Don't Rest on Your Laurels

Complacency is a silent killer, yet it's far too common. We climb from the trenches early in life, sweat and work and endeavor to reach the top, and once we get there we sigh with satisfaction, content with our achievements, and wait to become extinct. Success is a wild and crazy rollercoaster full of ups, downs, twists, turns, excitement, and fear. And while a rollercoaster ride is fun in the short-term, it's not the best way to live in the long-term if you want a healthy heart.

Success can become a problem if it's treated mainly as the means to an end. The moment you rest on your laurels, confident about your efforts, is the moment you become stagnant. Complacency is destructive because it's immune to innovative thinking and change. It fears new opportunities and is nonplussed by imagined hazards that threaten aspects of your career, marriage, and friendships.

Complacency finds a happy home with a concept called "rustout," something common in America. Unlike burnout, where you wear out your body and dull your mind, "rustout," according to Richard Leider and Steve Bucholtz, authors of *The Rustout Syndrome*, is the opposite of burnout.

"Rustout is the slow death that follows when we stop making the choices that keep life alive. It's the feeling of numbness that comes from taking the safe way, never accepting new challenges, continually surrendering to the day-to-day routine. Rustout means we are no longer growing, but at best, are simply maintaining. It implies we have traded the sensation of life for the security of a paycheck... Burnout is overdoing. Rustout is underbeing."

Complacency and rustout both lead to underperformance, apathy and unhappiness, but it can be avoided, both personally and professionally. Here's how:

... Identify your blind spots. The greatest danger in resting on your laurels and growing complacent is that it creates blind spots in areas of life that need to evolve and change. Assess yourself honestly and maybe ask people you trust to give you unbiased feedback. Create a list and prioritize. You now have your targets.

... Where are you vulnerable? When we engage in complacent behavior in our personal or professional lives we no longer think strategically about the future since we are comfortable with our past and current success. Thinking becomes short-term, inward, and narrow. Moreover, when we are impressed with our past performance, we tend to be blind to new threats on the horizon, heading right for us.

... Be a risk taker. There's a saying that goes, "Those who risk little *are* little and accomplish little." Achieving success comes by taking risks. Yet people who are complacent lack the ability to look for new opportunities. They know what's worked before and keep repeating those behaviors while the world changes around them. Their activity is fruitless.

... Kick laziness to the curb. Complacent people tend to be focused internally rather than externally. Their activity levels are constant. They lack the ability to upshift into a higher gear when the demand for increased action is required.

... Develop a new appreciation for your life. The best way to beat complacent behavior is to admit that the best life you could ever imagine begins this very instant. Stop waiting for the future to arrive and bring it on. Don't wait until your life is almost over to realize how great it has been! Stop taking your days for granted!

A complacent attitude will keep you from moving forward in life. Shake yourself free of such damaging behavior by building your self-confidence, committing to seeking new opportunities, and living your life with the courage that you are making the right decisions.

Be Authentic

Being authentic means you have connected with your essence and can act in alignment with that grounded place. Living an authentic life is a combination of being and doing. It's a state of awareness that drives you forward, motivates you, encourages a curious mind and prevents you from living in judgment or superiority to the people around you. If you are authentic you are aware of your beliefs, desires, needs, talents, integrity, and perhaps even the destiny you seek to fulfill.

Since being authentic brings many benefits, there are reasons to adopt a more authentic life right now. First and foremost, it will help you establish a personal brand, one people respect, admire, and remember, a concept discussed earlier in this book. People trust individuals who are authentic because they're consistent in their approach and delivery. Authenticity is a leadership trait. When you commit to it you will feel better about yourself and what you can deliver.

Here are some of my suggestions for living a more authentic life. Implementing them will make you more competent in your professional life and better-rounded in your personal life.

... Always tell the truth. Own up to your mistakes and admit your shortcomings. Your truth is what you believe and this transparency should be present in your life.
... Express yourself confidently. The ability to demonstrate passion, innovation, and curiosity is a courageous trait and one that will draw people to you like moths to a flame.
... Recognize what you desire. Stay in tune with what motivates and drives you forward. Such powerful urges should be present in your life.

... Know what you are willing to put up with, and what you won't tolerate. This might involve the way you work with others, your personal and professional relationships, even how messy you allow your office to become. Identify what you are willing to face and what is non-negotiable.

... Increase your perspective. Live outside the box. Improve your frame of reference by working to modify your thinking and consider other perspectives.

... Live gracefully. Develop the flexibility to deal with whatever life throws at you. A nimble mind and level-headed response to challenges are admirable qualities. Discover what you enjoy. Find your passion in volunteering, exercise, art, travel, reading or other areas. These activities have the power to bring us alive!

... Leverage your talents and strengths. When you understand and utilize your natural talents and gifts, you will find ease in your life. This is alignment.

... Stop trying to be perfect. Striving for the unattainable is futile. Gain awareness by seeing what *is* perfect and realizing you cannot *be* it.

... Use your gut when making friends, business connections, and professional partnerships, even when interviewing for a job. Follow your intuition. Surround yourself with people who share your values. It's key to living an authentic life.

... Make your intentions known. Intentions are the "why" describing how you behave. When you actively share your expectations, you strip away doubt about why you are doing something.

... Learn early on that every touch point you have with someone creates an impression of your personal brand. Be deliberate about the way you present yourself at all times. Have conviction.

... Guard your time. Realize it's your most valuable commodity. You can always make more money. You can never make more time.

... Get your needs met. Don't be afraid to express when you need to be taken care of. This eliminates manipulation and you are free to be authentic.

... Recognize and accept when something doesn't feel right. When there is a misalignment, your instincts will do their best to make you aware of it. Listen to them.

Authenticity is about being genuine. It is important to your future success because it will liberate you from the pressure of trying to be someone or something else. There is great beauty in living an authentic life.

Accept Change

Change is constant. In our modern world, you need to get comfortable with it. I believe you should change as fast as you can as a person—if it makes sense for you. At the same time, it's okay if you don't know what you want to do or who you want to become. As long as you're going in the right direction, allow the elements around you to help you make up your mind as you live your journey.

Like Kathy and Kyle, it used to be that you worked at the same company for your entire career, up to forty plus years. Today the opposite is true. It's likely you will work at several different companies in your life. It's even more likely that to climb the corporate ladder, you will be forced to look externally, rather than internally, for promotions and professional growth. Combine that with growing diversity amongst co-workers, a never-ending flow of new policies and technologies, professional struggle and conflict, and so much more—it sounds like a recipe for an anxiety attack.

With constant flux in the workplace, you also have to think about the change you will face in your personal life. There will be dead ends, peak experiences, incredible happiness and sadness, unexpected challenges, and relationships that begin and end. In the midst of this, you need an integrative sense of mind to keep your sanity.

Staying grounded is a crucial component of managing change

and capitalizing on all the components of who you are. It will always be a life rule, not an exception. Consider this information:

... Whether you have an appreciation for change or not, you must get comfortable with expecting it, sometimes at the most inconvenient times. Gaining this understanding will help you feel that the unpredictable is more predictable. It will allow you to handle change with grace.

... Transition is what occurs when you are faced with change. It's the part of the process that tells you it's time to move on, that you must let go of something. While transitioning is an action step in the change management process, it doesn't happen on its own. You must make a conscious decision to leave a part of your identity behind. It could be a job or closing the door on a relationship that no longer benefits you. It can't happen on its own.

... Change is comprised of six recognizable stages: loss, uncertainty, discomfort, insight, understanding, and integration. Think of Kyle's and Kathy's stories. They went through all of this. Different emotions accompany each stage and can run the gamut based on one's ability to negotiate transitions and how they perceive a current change. Think of it this way: The energy that has powered an outdated role, status, or persona must be released for you to move forward to what you will become.

... Realize you don't know for sure what the future holds. This is part of change. At one point you may be moving forward but don't yet know where you are going. This is okay. Not knowing where you belong because your next identity hasn't fully formed is a place of great potential. Embrace it and keep your eyes, ears, and heart open.

... Facing change means you need to step up, speak out, volunteer, raise your hand, and look to be included in what is happening around you. Don't be passive in your life. Be active!

... Reality is an illusion. Many of us are convinced that what we experience is fixed and unwavering. It's easy to feel reassured and have a sense of safety when life continues as it always has. But this is how rigid, stagnant thinking forms and it's not accurate. When you let go of people or events you've felt attached to, you can let go of the thinking that has surrounded them. You strip away the veil of idealism covering the world you have created, usually for your own purposes. As you dismantle this, you can focus better on your consciousness.

... Change requires support from positive people. Make a conscious effort to ditch the naysayers in your life. Get rid of people who discount your abilities, refuse to support your choices and decisions, or advise through fear. Surround yourself with people who believe anything is possible. Be open to interacting and hanging out with people who can bring you outside your comfort zone, people who disrupt or challenge the status quo or how you think. They can often make you into a better version of yourself.

My Wish for You

Throughout this book, I have focused on delivering a message. I know that you, as a member of a younger generation, emerging leader, driven business professional, and vibrant member of the human race, want to do all in your power to build a successful career and the life you dream about.

It's an ambitious, worthy goal.

But remember that your career shouldn't be your whole life. Don't define success by the money in your retirement account or the job title you attain. Don't pin a badge of honor on the number of hours you work, your ability to be constantly connected, or being so dedicated that you answer emails at two in the morning when you should be cuddling with your partner or spouse.

Someday when you near retirement, when you start to see wrinkles around your eyes and feel time creeping into your bones, will the money and power you've accumulated be enough to carry you to the next chapter?

Plenty of people who have millions of dollars in their bank accounts don't truly know their spouse or kids. Some build successful businesses and inhabit oak-paneled offices on the executive floor but forget to vacation, develop hobbies, and collect memories. They may not have a single friend they can sit down with to enjoy conversation and a bottle of wine.

So my wish for you is that you don't live your life in the rear-view mirror. Realize that to be truly successful, in your career and in life, your gaze should be focused on living in the present. Develop your interests, be aware of who you are and who you want to be, take time to be with your family and friends, surround yourself with people who complement and challenge you, be deliberate with your intentions, and always seek to adapt, evolve, and change. In retirement, it will benefit you just as much as a healthy bank account. Plan for the future, but live effectively for today.

Explore. Think. Change. Evolve. Grow. Laugh. Relax. Read. Work. Live. Discover. Do these things now, then be ready for what comes next.

REFERENCES

1.) Pew Research Center. Mobile Technology Fact Sheet. http://www.pewinternet.org/fact-sheets/mobile-technology-fact-sheet/

2.) Pew Research Center. Mobile Technology Fact Sheet. http://www.pewinternet.org/fact-sheets/mobile-technology-fact-sheet/

3.) National Public Radio. http://www.wbur.org/2013/01/17/digital-lives-itp:/www.pewinternet.org/fact-sheets/mobile-technology-fact-sheet/

4.) Pew Research Center. Couples, the Internet, and Social Media. http://www.pewinternet.org/2014/02/11/couples-the-internet-and-social-media/

5.) The Seattle Times. Companies take steps to prevent burnout. http://seattletimes.com/html/businesstechnology/2022387726_workerburnoutpreventionxml.html

6.) The Seattle Times. Companies take steps to prevent burnout. http://seattletimes.com/html/businesstechnology/2022387726_workerburnoutpreventionxml.html

7.) The Kavli Foundation. The Neuroscience of Decision Making. http://www.kavlifoundation.org/science-spotlights/neuroscience-of-decision-making#.VXsV_M9VhBc

8.) Gallup. Majority of U.S. employees not engaged despite gains in 2014. http://www.gallup.com/poll/181289/majority-employees-not-engaged-despite-gains-2014.aspx

9.) Psychology Today. People who are connected together work harder. https://www.psychologytoday.com/blog/brain-wise/201310/people-who-are-connected-together-work-harder-0

MEET RITA BARRETO CRAIG

If motivation and innovation are the life blood of business, Human Resources is the heart that keeps it all flowing. And nobody knows it better than Rita Barreto Craig, SPHR, SHRM-SCP. She taps into over four decades of corporate and global human resources experience to help transform clients—individuals, companies, public sector, and associations—into highly effective employees, executives, and organizations. Her style is entertaining as well as transformational and includes a client list of Fortune 50-500 companies in the United States, Canada, Europe, China, Singapore, and Latin America.

In addition to her professional accomplishments, Rita draws from her life experience as one of 11 siblings, delighting audiences with her inspirational outlook, anecdotal approach to business strategies, and irresistible charm. Passionate about inspiring and growing employee engagement, Rita has served to help organizations like Microsoft, Florida Power & Light, Office Depot, Pratt & Whitney, the City of Hollywood, Florida, and many more. She has delivered highly motivational keynote addresses and was a featured TEDx speaker in 2015.

Rita's impressive HR skill set has also been broadly recognized. She has three gubernatorial appointments and was voted by HR Florida as the top HR professional within the state. October 2012 dawned with Rita being presented with the inaugural Lifetime Achievement Award by the Human Resource Association of Palm Beach County—she is the only recipient of the award to date. She is active in a variety of organizations including the National Speakers Association and most recently served as the President of the Florida Speakers Association.

Rita currently lives in Palm Beach Gardens, with her husband, Steve. When she isn't helping the next generation of leaders find their true calling and live an inspired life, she enjoys playing a not so pretty round of golf. Rita invites you to watch her TEDx talk, engage with her online at www.toptierleadership.com and @RitaBCraig on Twitter.

ACKNOWLEDGEMENTS

I'd like to thank the many friends who have encouraged me to write this book. Your support, guidance, and wisdom is treasured beyond words. A special thanks to Anne Obarski for regular calls of support and to simply talk about every topic under the sun! To Fran Hathaway, thank you for your amazing thoughts. Your input greatly enhanced the book.

Thank you to all my clients. You have given me your trust and the privilege to work with you. I am forever grateful.

Finally, to YOU, the reader. I celebrate you for taking the time to invest in your future. Create the life you want. Learn from those before you. Never be afraid to try something new.

YOU'RE INVITED!

Rita "The Traditionista" invites you to visit her on Facebook and share your take on the power of traditions in your own life. No matter if your "tradition tale" involves your work or home life, go to Facebook today and share your story with Rita and other readers! With your permission, she may feature your traditions in a future blog post, newsletter, or book!

 /Top-Tier-Leadership

SHE WANTS TO HEAR FROM YOU!

Rita invites you to engage with her online and begin a conversation. Visit Rita online at www.toptierleadership.com or follow her on Twitter @TopTierLeader. If you are interested in booking Rita as a speaker or consultant, email info@toptierleadership.com.

NOTES

NOTES

NOTES

PERSONAL ACTIONS I WILL TAKE